I was the girl
with the moon-shaped face
—

Heather Lang Cassera

—

Zeitgeist Press

Contact the poet through her website:
www.heatherlang.cassera.net

Earlier versions of these works have been published in *Architrave; Back to Where You Once Belonged; Clark; Cider Press Review; Citron Review; Desert Companion; Diode; Hoot; IthacaLit; Legs of Tumbleweeds, Wings of Lace; The Normal School; Paper Darts; Red Rock Review; Rock & Sling; South Dakota Review; Watershed Review;* and *Whiskey Island.* The poet would like to express her gratitude to the editors and staff of these literary endeavors.

The poet would also like to thank her family, her colleagues and students with Nevada State College, her fellow Jellyfish (forever), her Vegas Valley writing community, the folks with Zeitgeist Press, her TLR and FDU MFA communities, the folks with Murphy Writing of Stockton University, Jen Tappenden whose dazzling prose inspired some of these poems, and the other brilliant writers who have and who continue to support and to inspire her. Also, thank you, Michael—always, and for everything. You mean more than words can say.

Cover art: Michael Cassera
Proofreader: Racquel Henry

ISBN: 978-1-940572-16-1

Zeitgeist Press
5771 Empress Garden Court.
Las Vegas, NV 89148 U.S.A.
www.zeitgeist-press.com

In loving memory of
Henryka "Harriet" Obremski Falkowski

When I saw my first
roadrunner, her legs were tumble-
weeds & her wings,
      drenched lace.

1.

I was the girl with the moon-
shaped face. Beyond my window,

tiny starflowers bloomed.
Downstairs, plates shattered,

& I wished they would fall,
if they must fall, something more

like petals,
& I'd whisper,

faith gets you to heaven.
I tried to connect those dots,

but I already preferred
the gasping stars.

2.

We stopped holding hands, little brother,
when it became clear that we could not be saved.

If the tooth fairy were not real,
& Saint Nicholas was something

more like our father,
then there could be no God.

You were my little brother,
but I believed in you.

You were glad that you refused to leave
your molars, those enamel-coated nerves,

beneath your pillow
especially for someone impossible.

Teeth are covered with the strongest
tissues in our bodies,

but even these we give up so easily.
You were four when you told me

you were seven, & I asked,
Where have five & six gone?

You pointed toward the mountains
of winter jackets & photos of our older sister,

the one we will never meet.
These tangible images

were clipped to wires & strung across the wall.
Even then, we were already pretending

that there were silver linings
without the clouds.

3.

Our mother was unquiet.
The words in her throat

were too cautious
to survive.

The lamp glanced
downward, the

light
collapsed

at her feet.
It had been years

since she lost her daughter,
but her thoughts remained

above the terra-
cotta roof, italicized

amongst the bone-
white clouds

as hollow as
the winged structures

of flight-
less birds.

At night our sprinklers brimmed,
  & strands of water crossed each other
like knitting needles.

4.

What if we could have
measured minutes with yarn,

not only with the tick
of each pebble against

our first-grade teacher's heavy door,
the kind with damper & spring

meant to slow the closing.
We thought there was something pretty

about bone, the intricate lattice & lace.
There was so much we did not yet know:

the calcium carbonate & phosphate,
& that sometimes there is loss.

Back then, we were young.
We were sitting in a tree.

We had heard of the word *fragile*,
but we had thought it meant glass,

even as we held together
our own construction paper & glue.

Who knew there were other things
that could not fall more than once.

5.

As if from a nest,
our exhales would fall to the sky,

but lungs are not quite hearts—
they are in pairs, & always empty,

even when full.
The sun would slip up

the side of our home
even though our house had gravity.

We never really knew
our neighbors,

& the shadow-tide
of our scalloped tile-roof

would lower itself down
the cinderblock divide,

& the trellised pergola
would swallow up my small body.

We can still find that
sun-drenched & abandoned cage

just beyond the swings
whose rise & whose fall stopped

sometime before me,
& sometime

after my sister
became gone.

6.

I opened the curtain
in my bedroom, just in case,

& that night a pair of deer
came to my window.

For minutes, they did not move.
They also did not seem to be afraid.

If I had run more quickly,
maybe my crescent feet

could have capsized the dark earth,
if only for a moment, if only

in my backyard, if only in our garden
that refused to grow without tangling.

Bedtime stories & origin myths,
the two are not the same.

How could I fail
to understand this?

Later that night, it snowed,
& I was cold, & I was still

thinking about how some blankets
aren't warm, & I was still

looking for harbingers
of yesterdays,

& I was still hoping
that my own fallopian antlers

might someday become branches
& then hollow,

& then something unspeakable &
then two hidden lungs.

We would pretend that
each of our fingers was a songbird's spine
that would sing
the liar's narrative.

7.

The kitchen door was cracked open.
On a good day, we might have called this

our family's domestic fissure.
We could see hands, & only hands,

our father's, him washing his hands
which were only a few hues darker

than the porcelain of the sink.
They crossed over & under one another,

rubbing gently, & sometimes not.
Those hands were unanchored.

They were hinged to nonexistent
slackless lines. They were

fingers & palms, then feathers & wings.
They were also blunt.

Because of these memories,
little brother, I will always want

a birdbath in my backyard
despite, or maybe because of,

never having loved
a literal bird.

8.

When I was young,
I'd ask for Grandma Busha.

Pick one or the other,
the adults would say.

You don't need to say
Grandma Grandma.

But there's something
about redundancy.

Some folks put cinnamon on their tongues,
& they call it a dusting.

They call it anti-inflammatory.
To me, it's the soil of certain memories,

sprinkled over sugar & over butter
& on top of Wonder Bread.

It is something that is constant.
It is something that is passed down

from mother to child even though
we no longer speak the language.

Busha isn't Polish,
a man once told me.

Apparently, it's Polish-American slang,
& no one knows where or when it began,

but even when our throats
are sore & red,

we still toast
our cinnamon-sugar bread

because some things
need to be repeated.

9.

The teacup, $3.05 with bluebells climbing
the handle & rolled rim, was stamped:

Ivory, Walker China, Vitrified,
Bedford, Ohio, H-52.

It was to be a present,
but once home,

I noticed the crack.
It became a gift

I could not give.
I held the relic,

fingertips touching
almost like prayer.

I wanted to know small
& accidental happiness,

that *H-52* stood
for August, 1952,

a birthday of sorts,
& I wanted to know

a word, *vitrified:*
to have been made

by fire
difficult to break.

10.

There was a ghost bike
on East Washington & 2nd Street,

& it was stripped,
tireless.

For everywhere
we have been, we have been

there a first time.
A wasp shivered

& traced the shadow
of our dog

who was wonderfully
unafraid.

11.

As a girl, I imagined lungs
as a pair of inverted atomic bombs.

Even before the divorce,
I had wondered,

do *they* get sick of their togetherness?
Lungs rise & fall in tandem.

Beneath the desert sun, they play a game
of who-can-hold-their-breath-the-longest,

then rock, paper, scissors, lizard, BOMB.
Even then I knew that sometimes we see

what we are not yet ready to hear.
I remember the hand on my shoulder.

I remember the sign at the Trinity test site,
that light travels more quickly than sound.

Near the still-curing
        Hoover Dam, a helicopter's search
-light flooded the moon
                roof.

12.

We drove east just far enough
to be one time zone closer.

We stopped for fuel,
& we waded through

some sort of white light.
We pawed at cans of Campbell's soup,

a water gun,
a box of Tylenol,

& a superhero
Kleenex box.

We became today's
postmodern desert outlaws,

a strange vying
I would never wish on anyone.

I was silently drowning
one moment at a time,

& it was always to that same
goddamn *that's-not-love* song,

which still leaves me wondering
what is set to repeat,

but oh honey, yes, there is water,
still, here in the Mojave.

13.

Through a telescope,
scientists stared at the sun

as it was eight minutes ago.
What scared me the most

were the things
I could not remember

like the man across the room,
who was a copy

of my father
but twenty years older.

My mother's countertop was dirty.
The blue sky was covered in spilled milk.

My fists continued to hatch—
always falling short of the heart.

Luxury was the blue
scorpion, something

        like the sky, with a shell
        that was segmented

like wind-chapped
knuckles.

14.

Do you remember, little brother,
the night our goldfish

disappeared?
We woke up late.

You had taken the bed with the view.
I was nearer to the door.

It was almost as if sequins & flesh
had never swum between us.

The fishbowl was right
where we had left it.

You had called it globe-like.
I couldn't decide

whether the scalloped glass lips looked
as if they had been captured mid-bloom

or mid-explosion,
but it didn't really matter.

We tore apart our bedding.
We crawled inch-by-inch

across each plank
of hardwood floor.

No matter our efforts,
we could not find the fish,

& we did not have the heart
to name it after it was gone.

15.

The dotted lines pulled
our moving van up the incline.

In the valley, a thick lull brimmed
with faded-golden waves of dust.

Cars passed us by
as we talked about the view.

There was no turning back.
There were only one-hundred-some miles left.

Our ears popped
to the shifts in elevation,

& we sank beneath
the coral-colored red rocks.

The striations were distinct.
We held our breaths.

Our eyes counted the way down.
Ahead, there would be crags, too.

Perhaps a controlled fall
in love is the kind of kindness

for which anyone might hope.
We were anchored by the desert floor,

& our mother curled both hands
around the steering wheel.

She looked out & explored
the corsage blooms of the prickly pears

resting on the curves
of their cacti paddles.

We were making
our way home.

16.

Outside, the desert floor was a frame cracked open.
Abrupt landscapes, fifty peaks, were torn from the sky.

Inside, baked goods were readied for PTA meetings,
and babies loitered under tinfoil moons,

under sweets tucked in beneath aluminum,
anchored to the tabletop by gravity.

Inside, my own sheets were egg-shell white,
& they silently sang of surrender

& of being the place
that I could go when lost.

17.

I once was the girl with the moon
-shaped face, but I learned

the origin of the world
from the circus,

from elaborate beasts,
from sequins-covered acrobats,

who built
mirror-walled elevators

or neon rope ladders,
& who gave human intentions

to each jovial knot,
who murmured meaning

into every tongue-tied twist,
& into *look, ma, no hands!*

They were certainty,
& they were predictions, too,

but I sought the quick refuge
of quiet wrists & swollen heartstrings,

which were always crawling back
to the involuntary hollow of the heart.

Although circus clowns
      startle me, here even sand
blooms like confetti.

18.

It's the day before couple's therapy,
& I need a haircut.

The first haircut I want
is one that will make me taller.

I want a haircut that makes me look rich,
but not entitled.

I want a haircut that reminds everyone
of the color red, but isn't red.

I want a haircut that makes my husband
stop wanting to have an affair.

I want my hair curled: straight.
Actually, I just want it longer.

Give me a haircut with a strong oaken finish,
one that is party in the front,

but business in the back.
I want a haircut that is a single child,

but one that never gets lonely.
I want photographic evidence

of your best friend's brother's '80s perm.
I want a haircut that's politically correct.

Can they take a little off
the *in*sides?

I want a haircut
that makes the voices stop.

I want a haircut like a brick. house.
One that tastes like tequila

& will hold my hair back.
I want a haircut

that keeps the lashes out of my eyes
& writes Tramadol prescriptions.

I want a haircut that's nothing
like online dating.

I want a haircut that's noise cancelling.
Except for the *swish* of sideburns.

I want a haircut that just makes sense.
One that's $8.99 after tax.

One that doubles
as a mustache.

I want a haircut
that gives me something to believe in.

I want a haircut that holds me at night.
One that won't judge me.

I want a haircut that can frame my lover's face.
I'm a reasonable person,

but I have to draw the line somewhere:
I'm drawing it at bangs.

I want a haircut that wants fries with that.
I want a haircut that always matches my socks.

One that remembers my birthday
but forgets that I'm turning thirty three.

I want a haircut that makes folks forget
my maternal clock.

I want a haircut that wishes for world peace
but one that would settle.

19.

I was the girl with the moon-shaped face,
& I asked you, little brother,

what you wanted to be
when you grew up.

We both noticed the owl decoys, failing,
surrounded by birdsong.

We both wanted to change the world
without ruining anything.

I never wanted to be the dashing one.
I didn't need lightning to strike,

& maybe siblings will always be the only ones
to whom we can write letters

that would not be *I-love-you* letters
to anyone but us.

20.

Near Baker, along Highway I-15,
the world's largest thermometer

reads 87 degrees.
There are millions

of desert flowers. We slow down.
There's traffic.

You should know that
Zzyzx Road is exit 239.

This is, after all, all about the numbers.
We are 45 miles from Barstow

& another line that we shouldn't cross,
& there's one call box every mile.

It is California;
there are power lines

like giant robots with arms & legs
playing cat's cradle,

like when our mother was a kid—
something else I cannot remember.

It's 3 p.m. & brush makes long shadows
on the moon-like terrain,

here, in the desert,
a place where people shouldn't be.

Even layers of mountains
lose themselves, their detail,

due to aerial perspective,
but this desert is not high enough

for Joshua trees, & there are palm trees
where none should be.

We come up on Peggy Sue's Diner.
We have never been,

but we're four miles from Barstow,
& I ask if that's dust or fog in the distance.

I don't want it to be San Diego smog.
I say that it's okay to lie to me.

Four miles is fifteen minutes in traffic,
but it was never really about the numbers.

Heather Lang Cassera—a poet, critic, literary editor, and educator—
holds an MFA in Poetry with a Certificate in Literary Translation. In
2017 she was named Las Vegas' Best Local Writer or Poet by the
readers of KNPR's *Desert Companion*. Her poems have been published
by or are forthcoming with *The Normal School, North American Review,
Pleiades, South Dakota Review*, and other literary journals, and have
been on exhibit in the Nevada Humanities Program Gallery. Heather
curated *Legs of Tumbleweeds, Wings of Lace*, an anthology of literature
by Nevada women, funded by the Nevada Arts Council and National
Endowment for the Arts. She serves as World Literature Editor for *The
Literary Review*, Faculty Adviser for *300 Days of Sun*, and Co-Publisher
for Tolsun Books. At Nevada State College, Heather teaches
Composition, Professional Writing, World Literature, and more.
www.heatherlang.cassera.net

Selected titles available from Zeitgeist Press

Clark: Poetry from Clark County, Nevada $18.00
Trek To The Top Of The World by **Andy Clausen** $5.95
The Bear by **Andy Clausen** $8.95
The Cities of Madame Curie by **Laura Conway** $9.95
Joie in Chaps by **Joie Cook** $17.00
Some Angels Wear Black by **Eli Coppola** $13.95
You, Of Course by **David Gollub** $14.00
The Satin Arcane by **Jack Hirschman** $5.95
Ghosts Among the Neon by **Bruce Isaacson** $11.95
The Last Lie by **Bruce Isaacson** $14.00
Lost City by **Bruce Isaacson** $5.00
A Page and a Pen by **Rodney Lee** $14.00
The Last Five Miles to Grace, by **David Lerner** $12.95
I Want a New Gun by **David Lerner** $12.95
The Dead Artist Talks Back by **Vampyre Mike Kassel** $14.00
A Boy's Guide to Arson by **Jarret Keene** $13.95
A Page and a Pen by **Rodney J. Lee** $15.00
Sudden Windows by **Richard Loranger** $15.00
Cockymoon by **Jack Micheline** $18.00
All the Broken Fire Escapes to Heaven in One Room by **James Norman** $20.00
Uncommon Knowledge by **Whitman McGowan** $15.00
The Queen of Shade by **Sparrow 13** $5.95
Testimony by **Maura O'Connor** $14.00
And the whole time I was quite happy... by **Marc Pietrzykowski** $12.95
Westering Angels by **Eliot Schain** $15.00
The Horizontal Poet by **Jan Steckel, M.D.** $14.00
The Underwater Hospital by **Jan Steckel, M.D.** $5.00
One Bare Foot by **Charlene Stegman Moskal** $6.00
Babylon Graffiti by **Syd Stewart** $15.00
When There's No More Room In Heck, The Darned
Will Walk The Earth by **Chris Trian** $5.95
Cannibal Cafe by **Julia Vinograd** $8.95
Cannibal Carnival by **Julia Vinograd** $8.95
Cannibal Casserole by **Julia Vinograd** $8.95
Detours by **Julia Vinograd** $8.95
Evil Spirits & Their Secretaries (new edition) by **David West** $14.00
Dogs In Lingerie by **Danielle Willis** $11.95
Tenderloin Rose—All the Thorns edition by **Kathleen Wood** $14.00

Zeitgeist Press
5771 Empress Garden Ct.
Las Vegas, NV 89148 U.S.A.
Orders and other information at: **www.zeitgeist-press.com**